WORLD PAPER MONEY ERRORS

BY

MORLAND C. FISCHER

FOREWORD BY DAVID F. CIENIEWICZ
PRICING BY GEORGE & CHRISTOPHER LEBARRE

World Paper Money Errors

By: Morland C. Fischer

Paper Money Images Copyright © 2010 Morland C. Fischer
Select Paper Money Images Copyright © 2010 Neil Shafer

Published by:
Zyrus Press Inc.
PO Box 17810, Irvine, CA 92623
Tel: (888) 622-7823 / Fax: (800) 215-9694
www.zyruspress.com
ISBN-13: 978-1-933990-25-5 (paperback)
ISBN-10: 1-933990-25-2
Printed in China

Cover Design and Layout © 2010, Zyrus Press by:
Bryan Stoughton

TABLE OF CONTENTS

ABOUT THE TITLE PAGE

Pictured on the title page is a 50-pound Bank of England error note dated 15 June 1933. This note is commonly referred to by numismatists and historians as an Operation Bernhard note. At first glance, one cannot help noticing a high denomination British bank note bearing an overprint (in this case, the serial numbers) shifted at a steep angle relative to the normal face printing. In fact, portions of serial numbers intended for three adjacent notes are visible. Similar shifted overprint errors are designated by FEN (Foreign Error Note) Category 3 (with FEN Category 8 representing the most significant errors), an error rating system which will be described later in this book.

However, the error note on the title page represents much more than merely one example of a shifted overprint. During WWII, the Germans devised the plan, Operation Bernhard, in an attempt to damage Great Britain's economy. The Germans intended to cause widespread inflation by dropping 5, 10, 20 and 50-pound counterfeit bank notes from planes.

The counterfeiting process began in 1942 at the beginning of the war, under the control of the German Secret Service and Major Bernhard Kruger. Skilled Jewish inmate prisoners at the Sachsenhausen Concentration Camp, in exchange for scarce perks and the promise not to be killed, engraved metal plates as exact replicas of the plates used by the British in order to print the original Bank of England notes.

In April, 1945, the Sachsenhausen Camp was evacuated and 8,965,080 nearly perfect counterfeit bank notes bearing valid serial numbers had been printed with a total value of 134,610,810 pounds.[1] The paper on which the counterfeits were printed matched the special rag-based paper used by the British.

While Operation Bernhard, named for Bernhard Kruger, was never put into action, some of the counterfeit notes were sent to northern Italy to pay the spy Cicero and to fund the strategic needs of the Germans and their axis partners. The Germans dumped the majority of the remaining notes (and perhaps tons of gold) into Lake Toplitz, hidden away in a dense forest high in the Alps, 60 miles from Salzburg, Austria. Although the counterfeiters were actually destined to be killed to preserve the German secret, they survived as their guards fled ahead of the advancing American Army.

Some Operation Bernhard counterfeit notes, like that pictured on the title page, turned up in circulation. Although detection is difficult, it is said that a counterfeit has a dull look in Britannia's eyes, her lower lip is not full, there is lack of clarity on the cross at the top of her crown, the fleur-de-lis on the crown is not well defined, and the marking on the vase as well as the background against which the vase appears is not very dark.[2]

Since calling attention to the meticulously designed counterfeits was to be avoided, it is indeed a rarity to find such a striking error on a circulating note of historical importance bearing the highest denomination among the entire series.

The highly secret German plot to destabilize the British economy with this and other Bank of England notes was chronicled in *The Counterfeiters,* a 2008 Academy Award winning film based upon a memoir written by one of the forgers who survived the Sachsenhausen Camp.

---

[1] From "Wikipedia," The Free Online Encyclopedia.

[2] The Shekel. American Israel Numismatic Association, Inc., Vol. XXX, No. 6, November-December, 2007.

ABOUT THE AUTHOR

Morland Charles Fischer was born and raised in Philadelphia, Pennsylvania and currently resides in Orange, California. He and his wife, Hildy, have been married for 28 years and have 2 children, Dahvi and Brett.

Morland graduated with a B.S. in Electrical Engineering. He later earned a Juris Doctor and is now a patent and trademark lawyer in Irvine, California. He has been admitted to the Pennsylvania and California State bars and the United States Patent Bar. He is a past president of the Orange County Intellectual Property Association.

Morland C. Fischer has been an avid collector of small size paper money for over 13 years. He is particularly interested in United States star (replacement) notes and world error notes including those featured in this book. He entered the paper money hobby after his curiosity and excitement were piqued watching a late night telemarketer show a U. S. error note.

Besides his numismatic interests, Morland is an active tennis player. He also plays the guitar and writes songs, especially for family celebrations. He has been a regular speaker to professional organizations, elementary schools, high schools and colleges.

FOREWORD

Welcome to the hobby of bank note collecting. One of the first decisions for any collector of bank notes is whether to collect domestic or world issues. Once this decision is made, the collector must determine the specifics of his or her collection. The book you are about to read will be especially appealing to those who have world notes and, more specifically, notes issued with rarely seen printing errors.

Morland Fischer has accepted the challenge of assembling a wide variety of error examples from different countries. This challenge was made more difficult by his inclusion of both the error and normal note. Mr. Fischer's book offers the added dimension of comparing values of similar errors printed on United States and world issues.

There are vast differences in the availability and value of error notes produced in the United States and foreign countries. For example, U. S. errors are generally much more expensive and available than the same foreign errors. In addition, a rare error note is usually deserving of a premium relative to its more common non-error counterpart. Mr. Fischer's book addresses these and other important issues relating to world printing errors.

With Morland Fischer's book as a guide, you are invited to experience the excitement of collecting world paper money error notes. The hobby has many enjoyable hours of pleasure to offer. I wish you good reading and happy hunting.

David F. Cieniewicz
Huntsville, Alabama

PREFACE

Thank you for reading this book and your interest in embracing what is a truly fascinating area of numismatics. A book emphasizing paper money errors calls more attention to the shortcomings of international printing methods than to the success of governments in producing billions of high quality bank notes. This book represents more than just pointing out manufacturing mistakes. Because of their elegance and elaborate detail, many of the world bank note errors highlighted in upcoming chapters can be considered individual works of art.

Books have been published that focus on United States paper money errors. As far as I am aware, this is the first comprehensive effort to address foreign bank note errors. Accordingly, this book will include features not practical in a book directed solely to domestic errors. In particular, I have attempted to bring together the inherent beauty of world issues and the distinct rarities of printing mistakes. To enable readers to appreciate their aesthetic appeal, the notes pictured in this book appear in color. In addition, the face and back of most notes will be shown even though the error is visible only on a single side. For purposes of comparison, a chapter of this book is devoted to the respective market values of both United States and world notes having the same or substantially similar errors.

Wherever possible, both the error and non-error types are illustrated adjacently to make the error more apparent. Readers will then be able to immediately recognize the error and appreciate its magnitude relative to a correctly printed note.

It is hoped that you will enjoy this book and gain the sense of enthusiasm I have derived from this very special area of the hobby. My passion for collecting foreign paper errors has grown into a satisfying and fulfilling pastime that I have shared with my family. After considering the ornamentality of world paper money in general and the often spectacular errors in particular, perhaps readers will now decide to start or increase their own collections and achieve similar pleasures.

Like the error notes pictured in this book, significant ones are rarely encountered, often overlooked, and seldom duplicated; we should strive to make the most of our opportunities.

Morland Fischer

Morland C. Fischer
Orange, California
worldpapermoneyerrors@gmail.com

ACKNOWLEDGEMENTS

Special thanks to Neil and Joel Shafer, with whom my wife and I have become friends while writing this book. Your belief in me as well as your contributions and care were vital to completing this project.

Thank you David Cieniewicz for your continuous support and encouragement and for writing the Foreword to my book.

Thanks to George La Barre for pricing the notes featured in my book.

Thank you Patti and Jon for sharing your cabin in New Hampshire, where the first pages of my book were written.

Thanks to my wife Hildy whose time and dedication were invaluable in assembling the variety of notes that follow.

INTRODUCTION

The first question one might ask while reading this book is "Why would anyone want to devote time to writing about world paper money errors?" A more general question is "Why would a collector or dealer wish to embrace this area of the numismatic hobby?" While there are several answers to these questions, the first and foremost is simply for fun! Unfortunately, world error notes are regarded by many as an obscure area of numismatics and a small segment of the overall paper money hobby. In fact, even dealers who specialize in world notes never or only infrequently carry such errors in their inventory. While the seemingly more expensive United States paper money errors are quite accessible at any large show, foreign paper money errors are quite scarce.

A large part of the fun is simply trying to find an available supply of such world errors to collect. To accomplish this goal, I have solicited the assistance of my wife, Hildy. In this manner, we have been able to make our endeavor a family affair so that both of us can share in the excitement of a "find." Hildy has become so dedicated to her quest for locating world paper money errors that she has been awarded the honorary household title of Secretary of Foreign Affairs.

The search for world errors has taken us to local and national shows, to domestic and international websites via the internet, and even to e-Bay. E-Bay has proven very useful for enabling us to scan the world and gain access to a wide selection of interesting and often dramatic foreign error notes at reasonable prices. As part of the fun of assembling a collection of error notes upon which to base this book, we have been introduced to a small but friendly group of dealers and collectors around the world who appear to share the same exuberance as my wife and me.

Complaints have been voiced concerning the bland and sometimes unimaginative appearance of United States paper money (an issue that has recently been addressed more for the sake of security and thwarting counterfeiting than for improving eye appeal). The same cannot be said for world paper money. Whether it is simply for their vibrant colors and impressive graphics or something more, the allure of such notes should be appreciated by every paper money collector and dealer. One's excitement can only be heightened when discovering that these pieces contain rarely seen errors, some of which rival and even surpass the most significant and visually impressive errors found in United States paper money.

Another important reason for collecting world errors is value. It appears that the vast majority of modern foreign error notes can be purchased for well under $350. These errors offer significant opportunities for one wishing to enter the numismatic hobby without having to invest large amounts of money to amass a respectable collection as might otherwise be required had United States error notes been pursued.

Despite their scarcity and eye appeal, world paper errors typically trade for a fraction of the price associated with the same error found on United States currency. For example, the rarest of U. S. paper money errors (e.g., double denominations and certain national bank notes) can sell at auction for as much as $50,000. However, even the most spectacular foreign paper errors will rarely trade for over $500. A significant reason for this disparity is that

xv

world paper money errors have, to a large degree, been overlooked or ignored by collectors and dealers alike.

In recent years, there has been a surge of interest in collecting paper money. Although it is still a hobby, most of us hope to someday dispose of our collections and reap significant financial rewards. Even such specialized areas of the hobby as fractional currency, obsolete currency and Confederate currency have seen renewed vitality and increasing values at auctions as well as on the bourse floor. Elevated price levels for important United States paper money errors were solidified at the Taylor Family Collection sale held in July, 2005. Increases in the price levels for foreign paper money errors may not be far behind.

For one seeking a visually appealing, unique and currently inexpensive area of the paper money hobby, collecting and trading world errors offers considerable upside potential, enjoyment, and the opportunity to be a groundbreaker in an area of numismatics that, like other previously dormant areas, could be ready to explode. Perhaps this book will kindle an awareness and instill a desire to collect foreign paper money errors that will make the foregoing a reality.

VALUES

Many who purchase publications having numismatic content do so to ascertain, "What's it worth?" However, we sometimes forget that paper money often has intrinsic value because of its rarity, its aesthetically pleasing appearance, and its reflection of historical times. That an error is present, particularly one which is dramatic, can only help to increase the extrinsic value or price of any note.

The market or extrinsic value of any error note, whether it be domestic or foreign, depends upon a number of variables:

(1) The magnitude of the error. The more dramatic the error, the greater the monetary value to collectors and dealers.

(2) Eye appeal. Not all errors are visible at first blush. Errors in security features (e.g., watermarks) cannot be readily detected unless held in front of a light source. Errors in serial numbers are often overlooked. Thus, while the error may be important, in some cases eye appeal will be lacking. Having a significant error that also provides great eye appeal will generally increase value.

(3) The face value of the note. Higher denomination examples are usually printed in lesser quantities than notes of lower denomination. Therefore, it follows that an error found on a note of relatively high face value will generally be more valuable than the same error appearing on a note with a much lower denomination.

(4) The rarity of the error. Although well known errors such as small misalignments and ink smears may catch our eye, less frequently encountered errors are likely to be more valuable.

(5) The availability of the non-error note. Inasmuch as some perfectly printed bank notes are in very short supply because they are either scarce, old, or both, even small errors appearing on such notes may warrant an increase in value.

(6) The grade (i.e., condition) of the note. It should come as no surprise that error notes of high grade will have a higher value than notes in lower grade having the same error. However, for truly great errors, the actual grade of the note may be less relevant.

(7) The historical market value of the note. Current market values are often dictated by prices previously paid for the same or similar notes in private sale or auctions.

Variables (1) – (7) are taken into account when estimating monetary value, regardless of whether the error note has a domestic or foreign origin. In the case of foreign error notes, one additional factor must also be considered:

(8) The country of origin. A large number of error notes encountered while preparing this book originate from the Philippines, India, and some Latin American countries. While such errors are worthy of our attention, notes printed in other (e.g., Western European) countries where paper money mistakes tend to occur less frequently may command higher prices. Collector interest in locating notes from specific countries can increase demand and cause a spike in prices.

When considering the extrinsic value of the error notes highlighted in this book in view of variables (1) to (8), I came to the conclusion that these and similar world errors trade for prices that, by any standard, would be considered "cheap" or, at the very least, undervalued.

There are several reasons for the relatively low prices universally associated with modern world paper money errors:

• LIMITED INTEREST

Probably the most significant reason for the lack of meaningful appreciation in the value of world error notes is apathy. Some collectors are not even aware that such errors are a viable and desirable part of the numismatic hobby. Other collectors, when having to choose between domestic or foreign errors, elect the former. After all, we are far more familiar with our own bank notes and are quick to recognize and appreciate any anomalies appearing therein. Some foreign issues are relatively small in dimensional size which may discourage their acquisition. The face value of many modern foreign issues represents only a fraction of the face value of United States issues; therefore, some may choose to ignore world bank notes altogether. Because of language differences, it is often difficult to identify text errors on a world note. Not being intimately familiar with the various color schemes characteristic of these notes makes it hard to discern an error when one or more background color tints or entire overprints have been omitted or incorrectly applied. Because the hobby in general has been reticent to show overt enthusiasm for world errors, a spark has been lacking to ignite an incentive to collect these notes. The limited interest (especially in the United States) in pursuing foreign paper money errors has overshadowed their relative scarcity and inhibited the same robust changes in value recently encountered in other areas of the hobby.

• LACK OF DEMAND

With limited interest comes a corresponding lack of demand for world errors in the marketplace. As with any commodity, the fair market value of an error note is directly dependent upon consumer demand. Those primarily motivated by quick profits and rapid turnover have typically shied away from adding these collectibles to their holdings. In short, this lack of demand coupled with a relatively constant (but limited) supply has tempered price increases.

• LACK OF RECORD KEEPING

Another important reason for relatively modest price increases in foreign paper money errors is the lack of record keeping. That is to say, and with respect to historical market value [variable (7) above], limited financial history has been tabulated for sales of world error notes. Records (especially by serial number) have been compiled to track the prices of rare United States error notes. Auction results have been archived to list the hammer prices of a wide variety of these errors. Such records establish a floor or base market value for trading the same or similar notes in the future. With few exceptions, comparable records are not available for foreign error notes. Because such historical value data has not been typically recorded, there is little to set the starting prices for most world error notes. What is more, any dramatic rise in the cost of a single foreign error note or a group of notes may well be forgotten. This lack of historical precedent has hindered any consistent price increases for these notes.

• MINIMAL RECOGNITION

United States error notes are regularly featured at auctions around the country. Both printed and electronic auction catalogs include price estimates and vivid displays of error notes from the mundane to the superlative. Hence, the current market values of even common errors can be easily gleaned from the multitude of auction catalogs being distributed year-round. Moreover, auction results are listed at the websites of auctioneers. Books have been published with detailed information relating to the types and prices of United States error notes. The cumulative result of this activity is to call attention and give credibility to domestic paper money errors as a valuable collectible. However, these same auction catalogs rarely feature foreign paper money errors. Without the publicity and recognition afforded by auctions and other publications, the prices realized by world errors do not keep pace with those of domestic error notes.

Price ranges have been assigned to the error notes featured in this book on the basis that each is in uncirculated condition. In some instances, a price may appear to be unusually high. However, prices were chosen to indicate what should be the fair market value while taking into account the reasons described above for keeping prices low and understanding that conditions in the future are likely to improve (perhaps, in part, by virtue of this book). Moreover, the assigned price ranges reflect an extropolation of expected prices over a period of five years from publication.

THE "FEN" SCALE

As has just been explained and as will be illuminated later on, the current market prices for world paper money errors as a whole and when compared with similar U.S. paper money errors are considered to be both unreasonably low and, in view of their relative scarcity and often fantastic eye appeal, not at all reflective of true value as a collectible.

Nevertheless, an indication of the extrinsic value of world paper money errors will now be provided without having to rely solely on a dollar amount. To this end, and based upon the variables (1) to (8) described earlier, a scale has been created to allow readers to gain an appreciation of relative price levels at which these and similar errors might trade on the open market.

Tables have been published in which to categorize United States paper money errors. However, no previous wide-scale attempt is known to accomplish the same for world errors. Accordingly, the notes featured in this book are assigned a numeric value from (1) to (8) corresponding to the Foreign Error Note (or "FEN") Scale.

One variable not taken into account when compiling the FEN Scale is grade. While most numismatic books proffer a number of different grades and corresponding values at each, distinctions will not be made in this book as to grade. When applying the FEN Scale, it will be assumed that all errors appear on uncirculated notes. However, it should not be forgotten that many important error notes are circulated and may well have a high FEN number regardless of condition.

Assigning relative numeric values to paper money errors is one of first impression. Thus, it should be appreciated that the FEN Scale is a product of considerable subjectivity as well as first hand experience. The numeric values assigned to the foreign error types categorized below are not meant to correspond with similar errors found on United States bank notes. For example, and unlike United States paper money errors, mismatched serial numbers tend to be a somewhat more common occurrence on world paper money.

The Foreign Error Note Scale categorizes error types primarily on their magnitude, eye appeal and rarity. The actual numeric value (of the FEN number) assigned to each note in this book will depend on additional variables such as the denomination of the error note, the availability of the non-error note, and the country of origin of the error note. Higher FEN numbers are indicative of rarer and more significant error types.

An error on the face of a note may have a higher FEN number than the same error on the back. Errors on the face are generally easier to recognize by inspectors and, therefore, are often the first to be removed. Accordingly, a note bearing an error (e.g., a back to face offset) on its face tends to be relatively scarce and, in some cases, deserving of a higher FEN number than a corresponding error (e.g., a face to back offset) on the back.

THE FOREIGN ERROR NOTE (FEN) CATEGORIES

ERROR CATEGORY – FEN 1
Shifted serial numbers (minor)
Shifted overprint or underprint (minor)
Gutters (small)
Excess inking/smears (small)

ERROR CATEGORY – FEN 2
Mismatched serial numbers (1 digit)
Cutting or alignment errors (small)
Extra paper (small)
Plate (engraving) errors

ERROR CATEGORY – FEN 3
Shifted serial numbers (major)
Shifted overprint or underprint (major)
Missing serial numbers
Missing overprint
Underinking
Ink/solvent smears (large)
One background color or design element missing from back
Extra paper (large)
Face to back offset
Different (revaluated) monetary denominations inverted over original denominations

ERROR CATEGORY – FEN 4
Mismatched serial numbers (multiple digits)
Overprint missing from one side and printed on opposite side
One background color or design element missing from face
Gutters (large)
Blank back
Back to face offset
Obstruction intercepting significant portion of printing

ERROR CATEGORY – FEN 5
Multiple background colors or design elements missing from the face or back
Cutting errors (large)
Cutting and folding errors
Alignment errors
Inverted serial numbers (Type I)
Inverted overprint
Missing security strip/foil

ERROR CATEGORY – FEN 6

Wrong color ink

Mismatched prefix letter in serial or series number

Printed folds

Inverted serial numbers (Type II)

Multiple errors on same note (minor)

ERROR CATEGORY – FEN 7

Blank face

Multiple overprints

Inverted back (relative to face)

Multiple errors on same note (major)

ERROR CATEGORY – FEN 8

Identical serial numbers printed on different notes

Identical mismatched serial numbers printed on different notes

Different monetary denominations printed on opposite sides of same note

Different monetary denominations printed on same side

Identical faces or backs printed on opposite sides of same note

Face and back printed over one another on the same side

The Great (But Possibly Unreasonable) Disparity Between the Values of U.S. and World Paper Money Errors

O.K.—By now you know that United States paper money errors sell at higher prices than world errors. Nevertheless, some of the reasoning used to justify this price differential is simply erroneous. In reality, it may be difficult to explain the wide gap between the prices of foreign error notes and their domestic counterparts. Listed below is some rationale which has influenced the mindset of dealers and collectors and contributed to the belief that foreign error notes are less valuable than domestic errors. But, is this purported rationale legitimate, and is too much attention being paid to factors that may be misunderstood?

Quality Control

Many American numismatists believe that our source for printing paper money, the Bureau of Engraving and Printing (BEP), has continuously introduced stringent quality control methods while the same control standards in some foreign countries are either lacking or unreliable. Moreover, the perception exists that some nations with large populations and constant inflationary pressures print unlimited numbers of bank notes with neither the financial ability nor the means to prevent a correspondingly large number of errors from being introduced and reaching the public. It follows that world errors are more likely to enter circulation and, therefore, should warrant a value that is indicative of a relatively common and readily available supply, with respect to United States errors.

The Bureau of Engraving and Printing does take care to reduce the number of errors in its product, and its standards are very high particularly when compared with those of many other countries. Nevertheless, the BEP is not as infallible as one might think. Take, for example, paper money printed during the 1970s. Serious collectors of United States paper money errors will appreciate that error notes were unusually abundant during this decade (especially for Series 1977 notes) in all types and denominations regardless of the best efforts of our federal government workers. For many years, BEP quality control was limited primarily to visual inspection of printed sheets and thumbing through packs prior to distribution. Also consider that some of the featured world errors were produced by such venerable printers as American Bank Note Company, Thomas De La Rue and Bradbury, Wilkinson. Thus, it is unfair to assume that an error note must always have a significantly greater extrinsic value merely because it originated in the United States. In this regard, it must be remembered that the number of errors that come to any market commonly represent a very small percentage of the total number of notes printed. Therefore, many error notes are true rarities and should be valued as such regardless of their country of origin.

Scarcity and Availability

Because of a perceived lack of reliable quality control among many world bank note printers, conventional wisdom suggests that the corresponding errors should be more plentiful and available than their domestic brethren. Remember that United States paper money errors are often displayed at numismatic shows and auctions. In fact, many dealers who specialize in or carry United States paper money also have at least some United States error notes for sale. Auction catalogs are regularly replete with pages of domestic errors. On the other hand, these same dealers and catalogs never or only infrequently offer foreign error notes. Even world paper money dealers often fail to offer error notes. Few paper money auction companies feature such errors during live or on-line bidding. While it may be that these pieces may be more accessible in countries outside the United States, they simply do not flourish here. Perhaps it is because of the efforts of world governments to improve printing safeguards that foreign error notes have become a scarce commodity. As governments care more about quality control and printing techniques universally improve, there appears to be a shrinking supply of world errors to feed the appetites of collectors and sellers. This paucity of foreign errors in the domestic market should, in theory, drive prices higher and at a rate which is at least proportional to the rate at which the prices have increased for United States errors.

UNFAMILIARITY WITH DRAMATIC FOREIGN PAPER MONEY ERRORS

Because foreign error notes are relatively scarce in the United States and have been almost invisible in auction catalogs, many dealers and collectors are oblivious to their variety and magnitude. Accordingly, it is hoped that the notes illustrated in this book will dispel any notion that the most visibly impressive paper money errors are limited to those printed in this country. In any event, readers will now have a visual perspective to decide whether foreign error notes should be added to their wanted lists.

COMPARISON OF SIMILAR UNITED STATES AND WORLD PAPER MONEY ERRORS AND THEIR RESPECTIVE MARKET VALUES

Monetary (i.e., extrinsic) values will be provided for the error notes featured in this book. For purposes of comparison, a sampling of selected United States and world notes bearing the same type of error are illustrated with the approximate market value of each. These examples will enable readers to appreciate the price disparity between U. S. and foreign error notes for both dramatic and simple errors.

CUTTING AND REAR FOLDOVER WITH LARGE SELVAGE (FEN 5)
United States 1969C, $10 valued at $1,000-2,000
Mexico 500 Pesos (P-69) valued at $200-300

LARGE PRINTED FOLD OVER FACE (FEN 6)
United States 1985, $10 valued at $500-700
Argentina 1 Peso (P-287) valued at $200-300

OVERPRINT (SERIAL NUMBERS) MISSING FROM FACE (FEN 3)
United States 1981, $5 valued at $300-400
Venezuela 10 Bolivares (P-61b) valued at $150-250

FULL DARK FRONT-TO-BACK WET INK TRANSFER (FEN 3)
United States 1995, $1 valued at $200-400
India 500 Rupees (P-92) valued at $200-300

2-DIGIT MISMATCHED SERIAL NUMBER (FEN 4)
United States 2001, $1 valued at $600-800
Great Britain 1 Pound (P-373c) valued at $400-600

SERIAL NUMBERS AND SIGNATURES INVERTED ON FACE (FEN 6)
United States 1935D, $1 Silver Certificate valued at $1,000-1,500
Brazil 100,000 Cruzeiros (P-235a) valued at $250-350

LARGE FOLD OVER SHOWING 2 NOTES ON BACK (FEN 5)
United States 1950A, $5 valued at $400-750
Canada 1 Dollar (P-85) valued at $400-750

MISMATCHED PREFIX LETTER IN SERIAL NUMBER (FEN 6)
United States 1976, $2 valued at $500-750
Philippines 500 Pisos (P-185b) valued at $150-250

SERIAL NUMBERS SHIFTED HORIZONTALLY ACROSS FACE (FEN 3)
United States 1977, $5 valued at $300-400
Nigeria 5 Naira (P-32) valued at $100-200

SOLVENT SMEAR ACROSS FACE (FEN 5)
United States 1988A, $5 valued at $150-250
Malaya 1 Dollar (P-M5c) valued at $50-75

WORLD ERROR NOTE EXAMPLES BY FEN CATEGORY

A variety of world error note examples and their non-error counterparts are now presented by error category. A FEN number has been assigned to each note with respect to the FEN scale listed earlier. A brief description of the cause of each error category is also presented. Because different countries may employ different printing methods and equipment, it will not be possible to completely explain every mistake. It will be assumed that the majority of foreign issues illustrated herein are printed by way of an inked (e.g., steel) plate in which a design has been carefully engraved. A sheet of currency paper is fed into alignment with the inked plate and then subjected to extreme pressure by an impression cylinder or similar roller within a press. As the sheet is forced against the plate, the inked design is pressed into one side of the currency paper. Such a printing technique is commonly referred to as the intaglio method and is employed by the Bureau of Engraving and Printing for printing today's Federal Reserve notes in the United States. Once printed, the sheet is then typically placed within a stack of similarly printed sheets and removed to a cutting stage to be cut by sharp blades so that individual notes can be made ready for circulation.

The size of most bank notes illustrated in upcoming chapters has been reduced to approximately 50-60 percent of actual size. The error note is shown at the top of each page. Wherever practical, the normal note is positioned immediately below the error. The opposite (i.e., non-error) side of the note is shown at the bottom of the page. In addition to a FEN number, the country of origin, date (or series) of issue, denomination, and pick number (according to the *Standard Catalog of World Paper Money*) are provided for each error note.

OVERPRINT/UNDERPRINT SHIFT ERRORS

Nicaragua, 1985, 10 Cordobas, P-151
Value: $75-100

An overprint consists of a serial number, seal, facsimile signature, date or denomination applied over the earlier printed face or back design of a note. An underprint includes one or more colors (i.e., tints) and designs applied to the face or back before the basic design or overprint is added. A shifted overprint or underprint is actually a vertical or horizontal misalignment with respect to the normal face or back printings. This error may occur when a sheet of currency paper is fed into the press at an angle or off-center relative to the intended axis of travel through the press. To a lesser degree, a shift in the underprint or overprint applied by today's methods may also occur if the press is stopped (e.g., as a consequence of an equipment malfunction or power failure) and then restarted or if a sheet is either accelerated or retarded so as to receive its overprint or underprint earlier or later than expected.

Error Note, Front

Non-Error Note, Front

Philippines, 1912, 5 Pesos, P-7a
FEN3 Pink background tint shifted left
Value: $400-600

Error Note, Back

Error Note, Front

Uruguay, 1887, 50 Centavos, P-A896
*FEN3 The signature overprint has been applied at a
steep angle across the face of this 19th century note*
Value: $300-500

Error Note, Back

Error Note, Front

Morocco, 1943, 100 Francs, P-27
FEN3 The overprint is shifted right on this colorful North African issue
Value: $300-500

Error Note, Back

26

Error Note, Front

Non-Error Note, Front

Columbia, 1986, 2,000 Pesos, P-430d
FEN3 Dramatically skewed serial number at bottom
with serial number at the top missing
Value: $100-200

Error Note, Back

Error Note, Front

Non-Error Note, Front

Germany, 1921, 50 Pfennig, Notgeld (Town of Oldenburg)
FEN3 Red overprint shifted up
Value: $50-75

Error Note, Back

Error Note, Front

Non-Error Note, Front

French West Africa, 1942, 5 Francs, P-28a
FEN3 Entire face design shifted down relative to background color
Value: $50-75

Error Note, Back

Error Note, Front

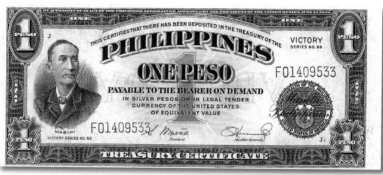

Non-Error Note, Front

Philippines, No Date, 1 Peso, P-94
FEN3 The overprinted seal is shifted left on this WWII Victory Series note issued October 20, 1944 to celebrate General MacArthur's landing at Layte
Value: $200-300

Error Note, Back

Error Note, Front

Non-Error Note, Front

Mexico, 2000, 100 Pesos, P-118
FEN3 Serial number at left is shifted up
Serial numbers from adjacent notes show
Value: $100-150

Error Note, Back

Error Note, Front

Non-Error Note, Front

Philippines, No Date, 5 Piso, P-160c
FEN3 Both serial numbers shifted down
Serial numbers from adjacent notes show
Value: $150-200

Error Note, Back

INVERTED FACES/BACKS

Germany, 1923, 100 Pfennig, Notgeld (Bremen issue)
Value: $100-150

In the majority of cases, the face and back of today's paper money are printed one after the other by different printing presses. Occasionally, one sheet or a group of sheets may be inadvertently rotated 180 degrees as the sheets move from one press to the next. In this case, the original leading edge of a sheet now becomes its trailing edge. In the event that one side of the sheet has already been printed, the design printed on the opposite side will be inverted with respect to its intended orientation. Therefore, each note cut from the sheet will have a face and a back aligned upside down relative to one another. In some instances, like the example shown above, rotating the sheet causes parts of two different notes to appear on one side of each note cut from the sheet. While considered a single mistake, this example is often referred to as a "Type II" invert error.

Error Note, Back

United States, No Date, 5 Dollars, Series 611, Military Payment Certificate
FEN7 An extremely rare inverted back on an "MPC"
One of perhaps three notes known
Value: $7,500-10,000

Error Note, Front

Error Note, Back

Non-Error Note, Back

Canada, 1986, 5 Dollars, P-95c
FEN7 Inverted back
Value: $1,000-2,000

Error Note, Front

Error Note, Back

Ukraine, 1992, 20 Hryvan, P-107
FEN7 Inverted back
Note that the serial numbers are inverted on the face adjacent the Lviv opera house
Value: $200-300

Error Note, Front

Error Note, Back

Mexico, 1972, 100 Pesos, P-61h
FEN7 Inverted back
Value: $200-300

Error Note, Front

Error Note, Back

Pakistan, 2006, 100 Rupees, P-48
FEN7 A rare Type II inverted back showing parts of different notes
Value: $300-500

Error Note, Front

Error Note, Back

Non-Error Note, Back

Greece, 1944, 2,000 Drachmai, P-133b
FEN7 Another rare Type II inverted back showing parts of different notes
Value: $250-350

Error Note, Front

INVERTED OVERPRINTS

Latvia (City of Libau), 1915, 50 Kopeks
Value: $250-350

An overprint (e.g., a serial number, seal, facsimile signature, date or denomination) is applied over the earlier printed face (or back) of a note. Like an inverted face or back, an inverted overprint error occurs when one sheet or a stack of sheets is fed into the overprinting press after being inadvertently rotated by 180 degrees. Thus, the original leading edge of a sheet now becomes its trailing edge. In different examples in this section, the inverted overprint consists of a revised numerical denomination printed upside down over the previously printed original denomination when it became necessary for a country to quickly change the value of its currency because of economic and/or political turmoil.

Error Note, Front

Non-Error Note, Front

Brazil, No Date, 1 Real, P-243Af
FEN6 Inverted serial number and signatures
(Type II) Parts of different notes showing
Value: $250-350

Error Note, Back

Error Note, Front

Non-Error Note, Front

Brazil, No Date, 2 Reais, P-249
FEN6 Inverted serial number and signatures
(Type II) Parts of different notes showing
Value: $250-350

Error Note, Back

Error Note, Front

Non-Error Note, Front

Brazil, No Date, 10 Reais, P-245Ag
FEN6 Inverted serial number and signatures
(Type II) Excess selvage showing at bottom
Value: $250-350

Error Note, Back

Error Note, Front

Non-Error Note, Front

Brazil, No Date, 50 Reais, P-246i
FEN6 Inverted serial number and signatures
(Type II) Parts of different notes showing
Value: $300-400

Error Note, Back

Error Note, Back

Non-Error Note, Back

Philippines, No Date, 1 Peso, P-117a
FEN5 Inverted overprint on back
Central Bank overprint on Victory series
Value: $500-700

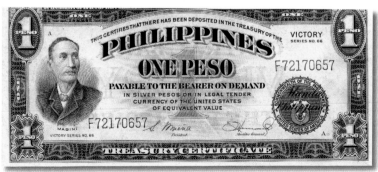

Error Note, Front

Error Note, Front

Non-Error Note, Front

Nicaragua, 1985, 1000 Cordobas, P-162
FEN3 200,000 Cordobas overprint inverted on face only
Value: $150-250

Error Note, Back

47

Error Note, Front

Non-Error Note, Front

Paraguay, No Date, 10 Guaranies, P-196b
FEN5 The signatures are inverted
across the top margin on the face
Value: $200-300

Error Note, Back

Error Note, Front

Non-Error Note, Front

India, No Date, 100 Rupees, P-91c
FEN6 Inverted serial numbers
(Type II) Parts of different notes showing
Value: $250-350

Error Note, Back

Error Note, Back

Non-Error Note, Back

Macedonia, 1996, 100 Denari, P-16a
FEN5 Inverted serial numbers
Value: $200-300

Error Note, Front

MISSING OVERPRINTS

Great Britain, 5 Pounds, P-378
Value: $250-350

A serial number is one type of overprint applied over the earlier printed face (or back) design of a note. The most common reason for a note to lack its serial numbers is when a single sheet of currency paper or a stack of sheets is not fed into the serial number overprinting press. Occasionally, the sheets are returned to the printing line after skipping over the serial number overprinting press. Where the serial numbers are applied last, the sheets may simply fail to complete the final overprinting step. To a lesser extent, the application of one or both serial numbers may be blocked or intercepted by an obstruction covering some or all of a note or notes on a sheet. In this case, the serial number is printed on the obstruction rather than the intended note. As will be explained in the appendix of this book, a note which lacks certain printing features such as its serial numbers may actually be a remainder, not intended for distribution, rather than a true error.

Error Note, Front

Non-Error Note, Front

Italy, series of 1943A, 10 Lira, P-M19a, Allied Military Currency
FEN3 Overprint missing from face
Value: $200-300

Error Note, Back

Error Note, Front

Non-Error Note, Front

Paraguay, No Date, 10 Guaranies, P-196b
FEN4 Overprint (signatures) missing from face and printed on back
Value: $150-250

Error Note, Back

Error Note, Front

Non-Error Note, Front

Saudi Arabia, No Date, 10 Riyals, P-23
FEN3 The serial numbers and signatures are missing from the face
Value: $150-250

Error Note, Back

Error Note, Front

Non-Error Note, Front

Netherlands Indies, 1943, 5 Gulden, P-113a
FEN3 Serial numbers missing from face
Queen Wilhelmina pictured on face
Value: $200-300

Error Note, Back

Error Note, Front

Non-Error Note, Front

Honduras, No Date, 50 Lempiras, P-66(?)
FEN3 Signatures and date overprint missing from face
Value: $150-250

Error Note, Back

56

Error Note, Back

Non-Error Note, Back

El Salvador, 1969, 1 Colon, P-108a
FEN3 Overprint missing from back
Christopher Columbus pictured on back
Value: $100-200

Error Note, Front

Error Note, Front

Non-Error Note, Front

Philippines, No Date, 100 Piso, P-164b
FEN3 Serial numbers missing from face
Value: $150-250

Error Note, Back

58

Duplicate (Extra) Prints

Bolivia, 1962, 20 Pesos Bolivianos, P-161a
Value: $250-350

Notes can receive a duplicate or extra overprint such as a serial number, seal, fac-simile signature, date or denomination in addition to the normal overprint placed over the face or back design. Similarly, the entire face or back of a note may be duplicated when the face or back is completed by a single printing press. An extra overprint may be added or a complete design duplicated when a sheet of currency paper is fed twice through the same press. In two examples illustrated in this section (including the example at the top of this page), a currency sheet was rotated 180 degrees prior to being fed (a second time) through the same press after the normal overprint (e.g., signatures) had already been applied. In this case, the duplicate signature overprint was inverted or applied upside down relative to the normal overprint.

Error Note, Front

China, 1926, 20 Copper Coins, P-S848a
FEN7 Different serial numbers are printed over one another on the face of this
very rare Tsihar Hsing Yeh Bank punch cancelled error
Value: $700-1,000

Error Note, Back

Error Note, Front

Poland (City of Lvov), 1914, 1 Korona
*FEN7 Punch cancelled note having a complete doubled face design
issued from a Polish town under Russian administration*
Value: $400-700

Error Note, Back

Error Note, Front

Non-Error Note, Front

Dominican Republic, No Date, 1 Peso, P-60
FEN7 Doubled overprint on face, only one of the two signatures doubled
Rare error on a specimen note
Value: $700-1,000

Error Note, Back

Error Note, Front

Non-Error Note, Front

Guinea-Bissau, 1983, 50 Pesos, P-5
FEN7 Doubled prefix letters
Another rare error on a specimen note
Value: $200-300

Error Note, Back

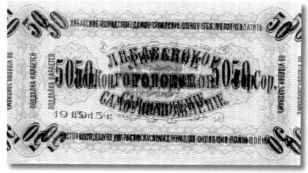

Error Note, Front

Latvia (City of Libau), 1915, 50 Kopeks
*FEN7 Entire overprint doubled on face of local World War I issue
from a town originally in Russia and renamed Liepaja in Latvia
Value: $500-750*

Error Note, Back

Error Note, Front

Non-Error Note, Front

Mexico (Monclova, Coahuila State), 1913, 10 Pesos, P-S631
*FEN8 10-Peso denomination printed over a sheet
of 5-Peso Revolutionary emergency notes*
Value: $1,500-2,000

Error Note, Back

Error Note, Front

Non-Error Note, Front

Bosnia and Herzegovina, 1992, 25 Dinara, P-11a
FEN7 Million Dinara revaluation
Overprinted at least 5 times on face
Value: $250-350

Error Note, Back

Error Note, Back

Austria, No Date, 10 Heller
Notgeld (Town of Offering)
FEN7 Complete back design doubled
Value: $150-250

Error Note, Front

Error Note, Front

Non-Error Note, Front

France, series of 1944, 5 Francs, P-115b, Allied Military Currency
FEN7 Overprint doubled on face
Value: $200-300

Error Note, Back

Error Note, Front

Non-Error Note, Front

Zambia, No Date, 50 Kwacha, P-28a
FEN7 Doubled overprint including different
serial numbers (710281/725000) and signature
Value: $400-600

Error Note, Back

Error Note, Front

Pakistan, 2007, 10 Rupees, P-New
FEN7 Different serial numbers (7399641/8815676) are
printed one over the other on the face of this modern note
Value: $400-600

Error Note, Back

Error Note, Front

Non-Error Note, Front

Costa Rica, 1991, 5000 Colones, P-260a
FEN7 Doubled overprint on face
Beautiful high denomination note
Value: $600-800

Error Note, Back

Error Note, Front

Non-Error Note, Front

Paraguay, No Date, 50 Guaranies, P-197b
FEN7 Inverted second set of signatures overprinted across the top of face
Value: $150-250

Error Note, Back

Error Note, Front

Non-Error Note, Front

Iran, No Date, 1000 Rials, P-115
FEN7 Doubled overprint on face covering the portrait of the Shah
Note that one overprint appears to have bled through to the back,
a graphic political statement at the time
Value: $250-350

Error Note, Back

Error Note, Back

Ecuador, 1920, 5 Sucres,P-S252
FEN7 The entire back of this lovely remainder has been double printed
Value: $250-350

Error Note, Front

MISMATCHED SERIAL NUMBERS

Zaire, 1995, 500 Nouveaux Zaires, P-65
Value: $100-150

One or more numerals of one serial number may not exactly match the same numerals of a second serial number overprinted on the face (or back) of a note. Serial numbers are commonly applied to a note after the face and back designs have already been completed. The serial numbers are usually added by a pair of counting wheels manually set and then automatically advanced as a new sheet is moved into position. To a far lesser extent, the prefix letter that begins a serial number or the suffix letter at the end may be mismatched from one serial number to the other on the same note. A mismatched serial number or prefix (or suffix) letter is sometimes caused when the two counting wheels are not initially set to accurately coincide with one another. In this case, notes on subsequent sheets will have mismatched serial numbers until the error (which is not always immediately apparent) is first discovered and rectified. A mismatched serial number error (like a plate engraving error described in a different section) is one of the few errors that may be introduced by humans rather than machines.

Error Note #1, Front

Error Note #2, Front

Great Britain, No Date, 1 Pound, P-374e
FEN8 Identical mismatched serial numbers (638-639) on different notes
Value: $1,000-1,200 for the pair

Error Note, Back

Error Note #1, Front

Error Note #2, Front

Scotland, 1978, 1 Pound, P-336a
FEN8 Same mismatched serial number
on consecutive notes caused by stuck digit
Value: $1,000-1,200 for the pair

Error Note, Back

Error Note, Front

Venezuela, 1986, 10 Bolivares, P-61a
*FEN8 Very rare non-consecutive 3-digit mismatched
serial numbers (xxx4x50x and xxx6x99x)*
Value: $350-500

Error Note, Back

Error Note, Front

Republic of China, 1919, 5 Yuan, P-125a
*FEN8 The face and back of this scarce note
bear pairs of mismatched serial numbers
Value: $700-1,000*

Error Note, Back

Error Note, Front

Error Note, Back

Non-Error Note, Front

Russia, No Date, 5 Rubles, P-35x
*FEN6 Mismatched prefix letters
(AY/YA) in the serial numbers
of a 1917 issue (old date 1909)
government credit note*
Value: $300-500

Error Note, Front

India, No Date, 100 Rupees, P-91
FEN4 2-digit mismatched serial numbers (304/234)
Gandhi pictured on face
Value: $200-300

Error Note, Back

Error Note, Front

Non-Error Note, Front

French Indo-China, No Date, 20 Piastres, P-65
FEN4 Two notes each having 2-digit mismatched serial numbers
(The cashier's signature is missing from the second note)
Value: Top Note $200-300, Second Note $250-350

Error Note, Back

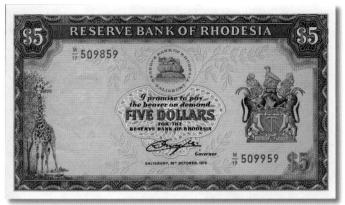

Error Note, Front

Rhodesia, 1978, 5 Dollars, P-32b
*FEN2 Mismatched serial numbers on a gorgeous rainbow note
from an African country now known as Zimbabwe
Value: $200-300*

Error Note, Back

Error Note, Front

Great Britain, No Date, 5 Pounds, P-385b
FEN2 Mismatched serial numbers
Value: $300-400

Error Note, Back

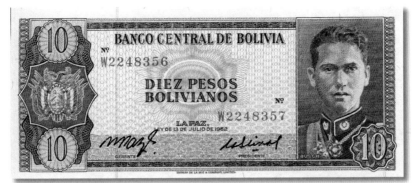

Error Note #1, Front

Error Note #2, Front

Bolivia, 1962, 10 Bolivianos, P154a
FEN2 Mismatched serial numbers on consecutive notes
Value: $400-600

Error Note, Back

Error Note, Back

Syria, 1998, 100 Syrian Pounds, P-108
*FEN4 A very unusual 3-digit mismatch of the Arabic
and Western/European serial numbers (1928999/1928510)*
Value: $250-350

Error Note, Front

86

Error Note, Front

Iran, No Date, 100 Rials, P-140
FEN2 Interesting mismatched serial numbers
in the Arabic numbering system
Value: $100-150

Error Note, Back

Error Note, Front

Bangladesh, No Date, 5 Taka, P-20a
FEN2 Mismatched serial numbers shown in Bengali
Value: $75-125

Error Note, Back

Dominican Republic, 1961, 10 Centavos Oro, P-86s
FEN8 An amazing uncut sheet of specimen errors
bearing inverted/mismatched serial numbers
Value: $500-1,000

The back of the uncut sheet of error specimen notes
shown on the preceding page

MISSING DESIGN PORTIONS

Philippines, No Date, 100 Piso, P-172d
Value: $200-300

A single design element or a significantly larger portion of a design is sometimes missing from the face or back of a note. A design element consists of a facial image, a building, a symbol, a numerical denomination, lettering or combinations thereof. Because design elements and larger design portions are usually printed during a particular printing, a single sheet or group of currency paper sheets may, for a variety of reasons, skip over and miss a press. The result of a missing design element is typically a small stark unprinted white area highlighted against the remainder of the normally printed design.

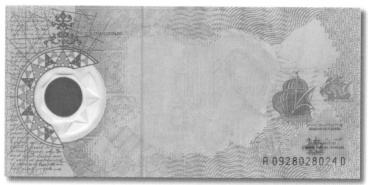

Error Note, Front

Non-Error Note, Front

Brazil, No Date, 10 Reais, P-248b
FEN4 Design elements (including the portrait of Cabral) are missing from the face of this transparent polymer 2000 commemorative issue
Value: $350-500

Error Note, Back

Error Note, Back

Non-Error Note, Back

El Salvador, 1980, 5 Colones, P-132A
FEN5 Complete design missing from back
Value: $350-500

Error Note, Front

K 0439703 A

K 0439703 A

Error Note, Front

Non-Error Note, Front

Zaire, 1993, 5 Nouveaux Makuta, P-48
FEN6 This note (and perhaps all the notes on the same sheet)
only received its face serial numbers
Value: $300-450

Error Note, Back

Error Note, Front

Non-Error Note, Front

China, 1949, 10,000 Gold Yuan, P-417a
FEN5 Design elements missing from the face
Value: $300-450

Error Note, Back

Error Note, Back

Non-Error Note, Back

Bukhara Emirate, No Date, 50 Rubles, P-S1035
FEN3 The black text overprint is missing from this 1920-1923 issue
from the Russian influenced Bukhara Soviet Peoples Republic
Value: $200-250

Error Note, Front

Error Note, Back

Non-Error Note, Back

Jordan, 1996, 10 Dinars, P-31a
FEN3 This note, which shows King Hussein on the face, missed its printing of al the al-Rabadh castle ruins on the back
Value: $250-350

Error Note, Front

Error Note, Front

Non-Error Note, Front

Dominican Republic, 1997, 5 Pesos, P-152a
FEN4 Design element (portrait of Sanchez) missing from face
Value: $350-500

Error Note, Back

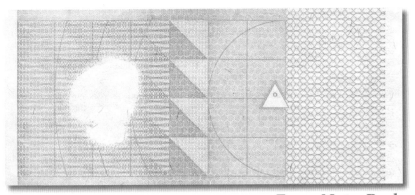

Error Note, Back

Non-Error Note, Back

El Salvador, 1997, 100 Colones, P-151a
FEN5 Design elements (including portrait of Columbus) missing from back
Value: $250-350

Error Note, Front

Error Note, Front

Non-Error Note, Front

Singapore, No Date, 1 Dollar, P-1d
FEN4 Background color missing from face
Value: $300-400

Error Note, Back

Error Note, Back

Non-Error Note, Back

Italy, series of 1943, 1 Lira, P-M106, Allied Military Currency
FEN5 Design elements missing from back
Value: $150-200

Error Note, Front

Error Note, Front

Non-Error Note, Front

India, 1992, 10 Rupees, P-88c
FEN5 Background colors missing from face
Value: $200-300

Error Note, Back

Error Note, Front

Non-Error Note, Front

Netherlands Indies, No Date, 1 Gulden, P-123
*FEN5 Design elements are missing from the face
of this Japanese occupation note*
Value: $200-300

Error Note, Back

Error Note, Back

Non-Error Note, Back

Indonesia, 1992, 10,000 Rupiah, P-131a
FEN3 Design elements missing from the back
Value: $300-450

Error Note, Front

Error Note, Back

Non-Error Note, Back

Colombia, 2002, 10,000 Pesos, P-453a
*FEN5 Design elements are missing from the back
of this high denomination example*
Value: $200-300

Error Note, Front

Error Note,
Back

Non-Error
Note, Back

Germany, 1921, 75 Pfennig, Notgeld (Town of Susel)
FEN3 Design element missing from the back
Value: $100-150

Error Note,
Front

Error Note, Back

Non-Error Note, Back

Brazil, No Date, 500 Cruzados, P-212a
FEN5 Design elements missing from back
Value: $150-250

Error Note, Front

BLANK BACKS

India, No Dates, 5 Rupees, P-80
Value: $100-150

When all printed features are missing from its face or back, one side of a note will be blank and appear entirely white. In this case, a single paper currency sheet or a group of sheets may completely miss or skip entirely over one or more printing stages in the printing line so as to emerge from the printing process totally lacking of its face or back designs. A striking example of a pair of sheets sticking together back-to-face during printing so that they fail to receive any design on the back of the top note and the face of the bottom note is illustrated later in the section devoted to miscellaneous errors.

Error Note, Back

Non-Error Note, Back

Thailand, No Date, 50 Baht, P-99
FEN4 Blank back, a rare error on a transparent polymer note
Value: $150-250

Error Note, Front

Error Note, Back

Non-Error Note, Back

Australia, No Date, 5 Dollars, P-51
FEN4 Blank back, another rare error on a polymer note
Value: $200-300

Error Note, Front

Error Note, Back

Non-Error Note, Back

France, 1973, 10 Francs, P-147d
FEN4 Blank back on a beautiful Western Europe issue
Value: $200-300

Error Note, Front

112

Error Note, Back

Non-Error Note, Back

Great Britain, No Date, 1 Pound, P-374g
FEN4 Blank back on another European issue
Value: $300-400

Error Note, Front

Error Note, Back

Non-Error Note, Back

Philippines, 1917, 50 Centavos, P-41
FEN4 Blank back on an emergency issue
Value: $200-300

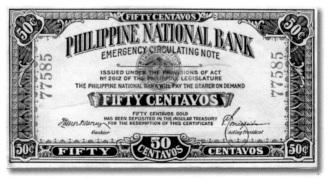

Error Note, Front

Error Note, Back

Non-Error Note, Back

China, 1945, 100 Yen, P-M21a
FEN4 Blank back on a Japanese military note
Value: $100-150

Error Note, Front

Error Note, Back

Non-Error Note, Back

Ukraine, 1991, 5 Karbovanstiv, P-83
FEN4 Blank back on a control coupon issue
Value: $75-100

Error Note, Front

Error Note, Back

Non-Error Note, Back

China, 1944, 1000 Yuan, P-J32
FEN4 Blank back
Value: $150-200

Error Note, Front

Error Note, Back

Non-Error Note, Back

Russia, 1994, 10,000 Rubles
FEN4 Blank back on an interesting private issue
Value: $50-75

Error Note, Front

OFFSET ERRORS

Brazil, 1923, 1 Mil Reis, P-110B
Value: $100-150

As the result of an offset printing error, sometimes referred to as a wet ink transfer error, it appears as if the face and back of a note are printed on the same side. Actually, one side of the note is correctly printed, while the opposite side contains both a retrograde image of the design intended for the first side as well as the correct design for the opposite side. An offset typically occurs when the ink on a newly printed sheet of currency paper has not fully dried. If the wet sheet is laid over another sheet, the bottom sheet may receive some or all of the inked design from the back of the top sheet. If the wet sheet is covered by another sheet, the top sheet may receive some or all of the inked design from the face of the bottom sheet. A note may also receive a partial or complete offset after a torn sheet, a folded sheet, or no sheet has passed through the press. This is the case seen on a pair of Mexican notes illustrated in this section which received partial offsets.

Error Note, Back

Non-Error Note, Back

Great Britain, 2000, 10 Pounds, P-389c
FEN4 Complete face to back offset
Value: $200-300

Error Note, Front

Error Note, Back

Non-Error Note, Back

India, No Date, 100 Rupees, P-91m
FEN3 Complete face to back offset
Value: $150-250

Error Note, Front

Error Note, Back

Non-Error Note, Back

Indonesia, 1980, 1000 Rupiah P-119
FEN3 Complete face to back offset
Value: $125-200

Error Note, Front

Error Note, Back

Russia, No Date, 60 Rubles, P-100
FEN3 The text from the face is offset on the back of this currency note
Value: $150-200

Error Note, Front

Error Note, Back

France, 1992, 500 Francs, P-156
*FEN6 The overprint is offset from the face to the
back of this elegant large size note*
Value: $250-350

Error Note, Front

Error Note, Back

Russia (Azerbaijan Soviet Socialist Republic), 1921, 10,000 Rubles, P-S680
FEN8 The inverted backs of four different notes have been offset at an angle over the normal back
Value: $350-450

Error Note, Front

Error Note, Back

Non-Error Note, Back

Argentina, No Date, 1000 Pesos, P-317
FEN3 Complete face to back offset
Value: $200-300

Error Note, Front

Error Note, Front

Non-Error Note, Front

Guyana, 1992, 1 Dollar, P-21g
FEN4 Complete back to face offset
Value: $150-200

Error Note, Back

Error Note, Back

Non-Error Note, Back

Indonesia, 2000, 1000 Rupiah, P-141a
FEN3 Complete face to back offset
Value: $200-300

Error Note, Front

Error Note, Back

Germany, 1923, One Million Mark, P-102
FEN3 The complete text from the face has been offset on the back
Value: $75-125

Error Note, Front

Error Note #1, Front

Error Note #2, Front

Mexico, 1959, 50 Pesos, P-49k
FEN4 2 notes (with cancellation holes) from the
same sheet each having a partial back to face offset
Value: $400-600 for the pair with letters

Non-Error Note, Front

130

See the letters that follow dated May 6 and 8, 1960 from American Bank Note Company with an explanation to company officials for "defective notes."

REQ'S WITH *aC* LETTER 5/9/60

American Bank Note Company
Garrison Ave. & Tiffany St.
New York 59, N.Y.
Finishing Department

W F C
MAY 10 1960

May 6, 1960.

SUBJECT: F 14087 - Banco De Mexico - 32/50 Pesos

Mr. A. Chrastil,
Asst. General Manager.

      Attached is a letter from Broad Street and two notes of 50 Pesos numbered H 1408963 and H 1418963, Serie 1A that have an offset of the back printing on the face.

      We have checked our records and find that the note in question was not a make-up. Attached is a 32/on lay showing position of notes.

      The passing of these notes was carelessness on the part of our Print Examiner. The Examiner of Numbers, employee #68529 Bertha Gallagher should have seen the defective printing as these notes were examined by the old method, every note was examined.

      We are of the opinion that the two notes in question were the only notes on this sheet effected by the offset condition.

      The notes in question were delivered 4/on and part of a delivery of 1,560,000 - 50 Pesos notes to Banco De Mexico, S.A. c/o Sucursal Eu Matamoros, Matamoros, Tamaulepas, Mexico, on December 2, 1959.

Examiner of Numbers Bertha Gallagher - re-emp. July 25, 1955
                     Laid-off   March 10, 1960
                     re-emp. May 2, 1960.

John Dunch
                Supt.

JS:MA
Enc.

REC'D WITH _____ *ae* _____ LETTER 5/9/60

W F C

May 6, 1960.

W F C

SUBJECT: F 14087 Banco de Mexico - 32/50 Pesos

H 1168963	H 1248963	H 1328963	H 1408963
H 1178963	H 1258963	H 1338963	H 1418963
H 1188963	H 1268963	H 1348963	H 1428963
H 1198963	H 1278963	H 1358963	H 1438963
H 1208963	H 1288963	H 1368963	H 1448963
H 1218963	H 1298963	H 1378963	H 1458963
H 1228963	H 1308963	H 1388963	H 1468963
H 1238963	H 1318963	H 1398963	H 1478963

American Bank Note Company
Garrison Ave. & Tiffany St.
New York 59, N.Y.

OFFICE OF THE GENERAL MANAGER
BRONX PLANT

W F C
MAY 10 1960

May 9, 1960

M. M. W.
MAY 12 1960

Mr. W. F. Colclough, Jr.
Chairman and President

J. W B.
MAY 12 1960

Re: Banco de Mexico
(2) Defective Notes (50 Pesos)

attached

    Please refer to letter from Mr. M. M. Wise dated April 29, 1960
relative to notes of the above with defective printing.

    Confirming our telephone conversation with Mr. J. Beckett of
May 6th, examination of the notes and checking our records indicates
that the defective notes were caused by a sheet printed just prior
to the one of which the notes returned were a part with a folded
over corner at the time of plate printing.

    A sheet printed in this manner would cause part of the impression
to be transferred unto the rubber D roll blanket. When the next impression followed the portion printed on the blanket was transferred
to the face of the notes from the D roller.

    We feel certain that only the two notes of the sheet in question
were affected.

    We are enclosing report received from our Finishing Department
and return the two notes, Nos. H1408963 and H1418963.

    - - - - - - - - -

Manager Manufacturing Division

AC:me
Encs.

cc: Mr. C. P. Foote, Jr.

GUTTER (INTERIOR) FOLD ERRORS

India, No Date, 10 Rupees, P-88
Value: $200-300

A gutter or pinch fold (sometimes known as a concertina fold) can be identified by a characteristic white streak or blank band that runs horizontally, vertically or diagonally across some or all of the face, back or, in some cases, both the face and back of a note. Prior to receiving its printing, a sheet of currency paper is sometimes pinched or folded over itself to create a closed crease that extends through one note or a series of adjacent notes on the same sheet. The normal face or back design is then printed over the closed crease while the portion of the sheet lying below and protected by the crease will remain unprinted and blank. At the conclusion of the printing and cutting operations during which individual notes are separated from the sheet for distribution, the pinch fold may be pulled open to expose the "gutter" that was previously closed and covered over. In the case where a note has a large closed crease area and a correspondingly large gutter fold when the crease is opened, the width or length of the note may stretch well beyond the dimensions of a normal note.

Error Note, Front

Non-Error Note, Front

Mexico, 1981, 100 Pesos, P-74a
FEN4 Wide "butterfly" shaped gutter fold affecting both sides of note
Value: $400-600

Error Note, Back

Error Note, Front

India, No Date, 1000 Rupees, P-94a
FEN4 Multiple gutter folds affecting both sides of high denomination note
Value: $350-500

Error Note, Back

Error Note, Front

Non-Error Note, Front

Iraq, 2002, 10,000 Dinars, P-89
FEN4 Wide gutter visible on both face and back
Value: $300-400

Error Note, Back

138

Error Note, Back

Non-Error Note, Back

Mexico (State of Chihuahua), 1914, 50 Centavos, P-S528d
FEN4 Multiple gutters extending horizontally
through the back and visible on the face
Value: $75-125

Error Note, Front

Error Note, Front

India, No Date, 10 Rupees, P-88c
FEN4 Another wide gutter visible on both sides
Value: $350-500

Error Note, Back

Error Note, Front

Non-Error Note, Front

Canada, 1972, 5 Dollars, P-87b
FEN1 Narrow gutter visible on both face and back
Value: $75-125

Error Note, Back

CUTTING AND FOLDING ERRORS

Canada, 1974, 2 Dollars, P-86a
Value: $1,200-1,600

Sheets of currency paper are cut into individual notes by overhead blades at a cutting station once the sheets are fully printed. In some cases, a sheet will be folded over or under itself after the printing steps have been completed but prior to cutting. A corner or edge of a printed sheet may be folded down or bent back if the sheet exits its final printing stage off-track or out of alignment with respect to the intended axis of travel through the press. When the sheet is ultimately cut into individual notes, the folded or bent portion is cut along with the remainder of the printed note. Following the cutting step, the folded or bent portion unfolds and shows itself but remains attached to the regular note. The result of a cutting error is a note that has an extra paper flap or "flag" which often bears a portion of the printed design from an adjacent note or extraneous selvage that was intended to be cut away. In this case, the width and/or length of the note may extend well beyond the dimensions of a properly cut note.

Error Note,
Front Folded

Error Note, Front Unfolded

Canada, 1954, 1 Dollar, P-75b
FEN5 Cutting and folding error
Value: $1,200-1,600

Error Note, Back

Error Note, Front Folded

Error Note, Front Unfolded

Chile, No Date, 5 Escudos, P-138
FEN5 Huge cutting and folding error involving large area of sheet selvage
Value: $500-700

Error Note, Back

Error Note, Back Folded

Error Note, Back Unfolded

Moldova, 2002, 50 Lei, P-14
FEN5 Cutting and folding error
Value: $350-500

Error Note, Front

Error Note, Back Folded

Error Note, Back Unfolded

Singapore, No Date, 5 Dollars, P-2a
FEN5 Cutting and folding error on an attractive note
Value: $500-700

Error Note, Front

Error Note, Back Folded

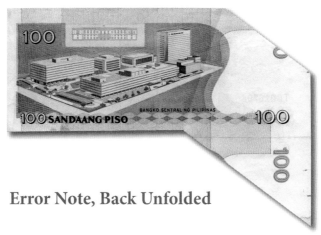

Error Note, Back Unfolded

Philippines, No Date, 100 Piso, P-172a
FEN5 Cutting and folding error showing parts of different notes
Value: $700-900

Error Note, Front

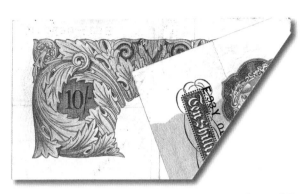

Error Note, Back Folded

Error Note, Back Unfolded

Great Britain, No Date, 10 Shillings, P-368c
FEN5 Cutting and folding error
Value: $600-800

Error Note, Front

Error Note, Back Folded

Error Note, Back
Unfolded

Argentina, No Date, 1000 Australes, P-329
FEN5 Cutting and folding error retaining selvage at bottom of sheet
Value: $400-600

Error Note, Front

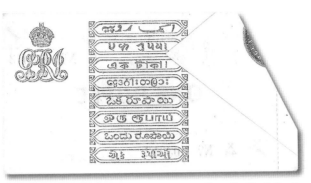

Error Note, Back Folded

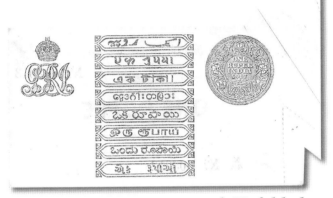

Error Note, Back Unfolded

India, No Date, 1 Rupee, P-1
FEN5 Cutting and double folding error on a scarce note
Value: $700-900

Error Note, Front

Error Note, Back Folded

Error Note, Back Unfolded

Turkey, 1970, 100 Lirasi, P-189a
*FEN5 A small cutting and folding error with
the biblical Mt. Ararat pictured on back*
Value: $200-300

Error Note, Front

Error Note, Front

Philippines, No Date, 5 Piso, P-168b
FEN5 A rare cutting and folding error on a replacement note
Note the unusual location of the [*] inside the prefix letter of the serial number
Value: $500-700

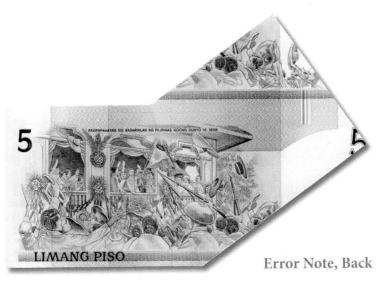

Error Note, Back

Printed (Exterior) Fold Errors

Indonesia, 1980, 1000 Rupiah, P-119
Value: $300-400

A cutting and folding error was earlier described as occurring when a sheet of currency paper is folded over or bent back upon itself after the notes on the sheet have first been fully printed. When the sheet is ultimately cut, the additional folded or bent portion remains attached to and stays with the note after it has been cut from the sheet. Sometimes, rather than being folded after the printing process is completed, a currency sheet will be folded prior to entering a press to receive its design or overprint. In this case, some or all of the design or overprint will be printed directly on the fold instead of the note covered by the fold. When the sheet is ultimately cut into individual notes and the printed fold is unfolded and revealed, the printing intended for one side of the note and intercepted by the fold winds up on the opposite side. A blank area is left on that portion of the note covered by the foldover prior to unfolding. Examples of a printed fold in this section include a printed tear where a portion of a sheet is torn and then folded over a normal note prior to printing so that the printing intended for the face appears on the folded tear instead.

Error Note, Front Folded

Error Note, Front Unfolded

Cuba, 2001, 20 Pesos, P-118
FEN6 Printed Fold
Value: $700-900

Error Note, Back

Error Note, Back Folded

Error Note, Front Unfolded

Venezuela, 1977, 10 Bolivares, P-51f
FEN6 Printed fold
Value: $700-900

Non-Error Note, Back

Error Note, Front Folded

Error Note, Front Unfolded

Pakistan, No Date, 100 Rupees, P-36
FEN6 Printed fold with printer's reject
Value: $600-800

Error Note, Back

Error Note

Non-Error Note, Front

Mexico, 1988, 100,000 Pesos, P-94
FEN6 Small tear folded and printed over face of large denomination
Value: $100-150

Error Note, Back

Error Note, Front Folded

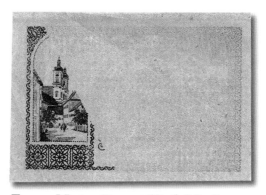

Error Note, Front Unfolded

Austria, No Date, 60 Heller, Notgeld (Town of Garsten)
FEN6 Printed fold
Value: $75-125

Error Note, Back

Error Note, Front Folded

Error Note, Front Unfolded

Bolivia, 1962, 20 Pesos Bolivianos, P-161a
*FEN6 Printed fold with unusual "H" shaped
marking printed along folded edge*
Value: $350-500

Error Note, Back

Error Note, Back Folded

Error Note, Back Unfolded

Macedonia, 2001, 10 Denari, P-14a
FEN6 Printed fold
Value: $250-350

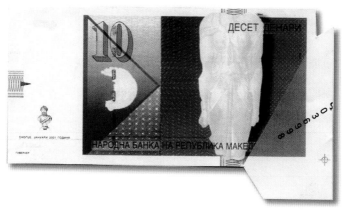

Error Note, Front

162

Error Note, Front Folded

Error Note, Front Unfolded

Argentina, No Date, 10,000 Pesos, P-306a
FEN6 Twice folded note with overprinting received on fold
Value: $500-700

Error Note, Back

Error Note, Front Folded

Error Note, Front Unfolded

Venezuela, 1986, 10 Bolivares, P-61
FEN6 Large tear showing parts of three adjacent notes
folded and printed over face
Value: $400-600

Error Note, Back

Error Note, Front Folded

Error Note, Front Unfolded

Mexico, 2000, 200 Pesos, P-114
FEN6 Printed fold
Value: $350-500

Error Note, Back

ALIGNMENT ERRORS

Austria (Town of Raab), 1920, 20 Heller
Value: $75-125

An alignment error occurs when the normal designs printed on the face and the back of a note are out of opposing alignment with one another. A first design is correctly positioned on one side, while a second design printed on the opposite side is off-center relative to the first design. In this case, parts of two different notes may be visible on one side or the other along either the horizontal or vertical margin or, in rare instances, along both margins. In some cases, depending upon the original location of a note on a currency sheet, the intended design on one side is shifted vertically or horizontally so that a blank or white area lies adjacent one margin, while the opposite margin is missing altogether.

Error Note, Front

Non-Error Note, Front

European Union, 2002, 5 Euro, P-1X
FEN5 A rare vertical cutting error issued by the European Union with large portions of adjacent notes showing
Value: $700-900

Error Note, Back

Error Note, Back

Ecuador, 1920, 5 Sucres, P-S252r
FEN5 A very rare error on an unsigned remainder from Banco Sur Americano with a misaligned back showing part of four different notes
Value: $900-1,200

Error Note, Front

Error Note, Back

Non-Error Note, Back

Russia (Azerbaijan Soviet Socialist Republic), 1921, 10,000 Rubles, P-S714
*FEN5 Parts of three notes of perhaps different size and
value shown on back and misaligned relative to face*
Value: $500-700

Error Note, Front

Error Note, Back

Non-Error Note, Back

Nicaragua, 2002, 20 Cordobas, P-192
FEN5 Vertical alignment error on back
Value: $300-500

Error Note, Front

Error Note, Back

Non-Error Note, Back

Mexico, 1973, 100 Pesos, P-61
FEN5 Horizontal alignment error on back leaving large unprinted blank area
Value: $125-175

Error Note, Front

Error Note, Front

Non-Error Note, Front

Korea, No Date, 1 Yen, P-38a
FEN5 Horizontal alignment error on face
Value: $200-300

Error Note, Back

173

Error Note, Back

Non-Error Note, Back

Germany, 1921, 25 Pfennig, Notgeld (Town of Zeulenroda)
FEN2 Small horizontal alignment shift
Value: $50-75

Error Note, Front

CUTTING ERRORS

Iraq, 1994, 100 Dinar, P-84
Value: $200-300

A cutting error typically occurs after the notes on a sheet of currency paper are fully printed. At the conclusion of the printing process, a stack of printed sheets is transported to a cutting station to be cut into individual notes. Sometimes the overhead cutting blades and the sheets are shifted or misaligned relative to one another. When the cutting blades move through the misaligned sheets to separate the notes, the result is that parts of two or more designs from two or more adjacent and independent notes will appear side-by-side or one above the other on the face and back of each note. The size of the adjacent design portions on each note will depend upon the amount of shift or misalignment between the sheets and the cutting blades. However, both sides of a note are similarly affected by a cutting error such that each side will show parts of different notes.

Error Note, Front

Non-Error Note, Front

Indonesia, 2004, 20,000 Rupiah, P-143
FEN5 Cutting error showing two notes with
different prefix letters in the serial numbers
Value: $600-800

Error Note, Back

Error Note, Front

Non-Error Note, Front

Peru, 1996, 20 Soles, P-169
FEN5 Horizontal cutting error
Value: $150-250

Error Note, Back

INKING ERRORS

El Salvador, 1996, 10 Colones, P-118a
Value: $150-200

A note will be under-inked when the engraved plate pressing on a sheet of currency paper does not receive a sufficient supply of ink. Under-inking may occur for a single color or different color inks, in which case correspondingly different design portions of a note will appear weak or faded. An over-inking error occurs when a surplus of ink is delivered to the plate or accumulates at a particular location on the plate. In different examples in this section, a solvent applied to clean a plate was not completely removed, so that a solvent/ink smear was produced when the plate was re-inked and a new sheet of currency paper was pressed against the plate.

Error Note, Front

Non-Error Note, Front

United States, 25 Cents, Series 471, Military Payment Certificate
FEN3 Major under-inking of the face
Value: $250-350

Error Note, Back

Error Note, Front

Non-Error Note, Front

Zambia, No Date, 50 Kwacha, P-33b
FEN3 Insufficient ink of face
Value: $100-150

Error Note, Back

Error Note, Front

Non-Error Note, Front

Indonesia, 1980, 1000 Rupiah, P-119
FEN3 Insufficient inking of the face design
Value: $100-150

Error Note, Back

Error Note, Front

Non-Error Note, Front

Great Britain, No Date, 5 Pounds, P-378b
FEN3 The Queen's Portrait is under-inked on the face
Value: $300-400

Error Note, Back

Error Note, Front

Non-Error Note, Front

Iraq, 2002, 10,000 Dinars, P-89
FEN3 Major over-inking covering almost the entire face
Value: $150-250

Error Note, Back

Error Note, Front

Non-Error Note, Front

Indonesia, 2000, 1000 Rupiah, P-141a
FEN3 Major under-inking of the face equivalent to missing design features
Value: $250-350

Error Note, Back

Error Note, Back

Non-Error Note, Back

Canada, 1991, 20 Dollars, P-97b
FEN6 Wrong color ink (green) used instead of normal blue ink to print back
Value: $400-600

Error Note, Front

Error Note, Front

Non-Error Note, Front

Indonesia, 1999, 50,000 Rupiah, P-139e
FEN5 Large ink/solvent smear across the face
Value: $50-100

Error Note, Back

Error Note, Front

Non-Error Note, Front

Egypt, 1978, 1 Pound, P-50
FEN3 Extraneous ink lines running vertically on face and back
Value: $100-200

Error Note, Back

Error Note, Front

Non-Error Note, Front

Peru, 1921, 1/2 Libra, P-S605
FEN3 Major overinking of the face
Value: $150-250

Error Note, Back

OBSTRUCTIONS

Indonesia, 2005, 50,000 Rupiah, P-145
Value: $300-500

An obstruction occurs when some or all of a note or notes on a sheet of currency are covered during a press run so that a printing originally intended for a note is intercepted by the obstruction. In this case, the obstruction, rather than the note, receives the printing (e.g., such as an overprint). Prior to the note being distributed to the public, the obstruction usually falls away taking with it the intercepted printing. Thus, the note is issued without its complete printing which often results in the face or back showing a blank or white area having a shape that matches the obstruction. Known obstructions consist of scraps of extraneous currency paper, a currency sheet that is folded over itself, and miscellaneous foreign objects, including chewing gum wrappers, bandage covers and currency banding paper that have been accidentally dropped or blown onto the printing line.

Error Note, Back

Non-Error Note, Back

Mexico, 1973, 100 Pesos, P-61i
FEN4 Obstruction intercepting design elements on back
Value: $500-700

Error Note, Front

Error Note, Back

Non-Error Note, Back

Somaliland, 2006, 1000 Shillings, P-New
FEN4 The serial numbers embossed into the
back were not printed because of an obstruction
Value: $200-300

Error Note, Front

193

Error Note, Front

Non-Error Note, Front

Great Britain, 2000, 10 Pounds, P-389b
FEN4 An interesting obstruction where one half of the serial number on the left and the entire security seal were blocked from receipt by the face
Value: $600-800

Error Note, Back

Error Notes, Front

Russia, 1919, 1 Ruble, P-81
FEN4 A large obstruction has intercepted some
of the face designs on a sheet of currency notes
Value: $400-600

Error Notes, Back

Error Note, Back

Non-Error Note, Back

Indonesia, 1994, 1000 Rupiah, P-129a
FEN4 An ink permeable obstruction appears to have moved across the back
Value: $250-350

Error Note, Front

PLATE ERRORS

Philippines, 2006, 100 Piso, P-194b
Value: $50-100

A plate error, sometimes known as an engraving error, is one of the few mistakes (including mismatched serial number errors) caused by man as opposed to machine. In most modern printing methods, an inked plate is necessary to the production of paper money. Manufacturing a plate with an elegant and complicated ornamental design requires a highly skilled engraver who must be able to accurately incorporate the very fine details of a drawing or portrait into his work. It is therefore understandable that an engraver may sometimes make a mistake, especially when one considers that the plate must be engraved with a mirror image of the design to be ultimately pressed into a sheet of currency paper. Because of the minute detail involved in engraving a plate, some engraving errors go undetected by both government inspectors and members of the public who may not be inclined or able to give the close scrutiny required to identify such errors. Some plate errors are caused by a simple transposition of letters, numerals or other details. Wrong letters or numerals also may appear on printing plates prepared especially during wartime or other periods of emergency.

Error Note, Back

Non-Error Note, Back

Philippines, 1942, 2 Pesos, P-655
FEN2 "FESOS" rather than "PESOS" printed on back right side
Value: $50-100

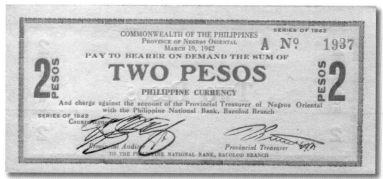

Error Note, Front

Error Note, Back

Bolivia, No Date, 20 Bolivianos, P-108
FEN2 "PESOS" rather than "BOLIVIANOS" printed along the border of the note on the back side
Value: $300-500

Non-Error Note, Back

Error Note, Front

Error Note, Front Close-Up

Non-Error Note, Front Close-Up

Greece, No Date, 500 Drachmai, P-109b
FEN2 "ENI" rather than "EΠ" printed on face to right of portrait
Value: $100-200

Error Note, Back

Error Note, Front

Mexico (Gobierno Constitucionalista de Mexico), 1913 20 Pesos, P-S632
FEN2 "VIENTE" rather than "VEINTE"
printed along the top and bottom margins
Value: $150-250

Error Note, Back

Error Note, Front

Non-Error Note, Front

Philippines, 1941, 50 Centavos, P-S632ax
FEN2 "Philipipne" rather than "Philippine" printed on face
Value: $100-150

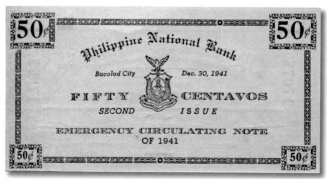

Error Note, Back

Error Note, Back

Error Note, Back Close-Up

Non-Error Note, Back Close-Up

Costa Rica, 1989, 5 Colones, P-236
FEN2 "T. VILLA" rather than "J.VILLA"
printed on back of lovely note
Value: $100-200

Error Note, Front

Error Note, Front

Error Note, Front Close-Up

Non-Error Note, Front Close-Up

Yugoslavia, 1978, 1000 Dinara, P-92a
FEN2 "GUVERNE" rather than "GUVERNER" printed on face
Value: $150-200

Error Note, Back

Error Note, Front

Error Note, Front Close-Up

Non-Error Note, Front Close-Up

France, 1992/1993, 50 Francs, P-157a/b
FEN2 "Éxúpery" rather than "Exúpery" printed on the face of
a note honoring author of The Little Prince, *reissued in 1994*
Value: $100-150

Error Note, Back

Error Note, Front

India, No Date, 100 Rupees, P-42
FEN2 The error note (black serial numbers) has error in Hindi in the value text on the face.

Non-Error Note, Front

Error Note, Back

The third line of text on the left side of the back is 27mm long rather than 40mm, as on the correct note (red serial numbers),
Value: $300-400

Non-Error Note, Back

MULTIPLE ERRORS

Iraq, 1992, 5 Dinars, P-80
Value: $200-300

Some of the most visually dramatic notes occur when an example experiences more than a single error. Multiple errors appearing on the same note are not typically related to one another and usually occur during different stages of the printing operation. While single errors on world bank notes are scarce in and of themselves, multiple errors are indeed rare and justify a high numerical value on the FEN scale, even in cases where the individual errors are relatively common when occurring separately. Nevertheless, a distinction is made in the FEN scale for notes having significant multiple errors. In one example in this section, three entirely different errors appear on each of a pair of consecutive 100 Yuan Chinese notes. Such multiple errors must be regarded as an extremely unlikely and random occurrence regardless of the country in which the notes are printed.

Error Note, Front

Non-Error Note, Front

Austria, 1920, 20 Heller, Notgeld (Town of Raab)
FEN7 Background color on face and complete text on back printed twice
Value: $150-200

Error Note, Back

Error Note, Front

Error Note, Back

Greece, 1943, 50 Drachmai, P-121
*FEN7 Face missing background color and
blank back receiving partial face printing*
Value: $300-400

Non-Error Note
Front and Back

Error Note, Back

Error Note, Front

Indonesia, 1992, 500 Rupiah P-128
FEN7 Face and back blank except for serial numbers on back
Value: $300-500

Non-Error Note
Back and Front

Error Note, Front

Error Note, Back

Columbia, 1900, 1 Peso, P-S504
FEN7 The overprint on the face is doubled and
the back is blank except for a partial offset of the face
Value: $500-700

Non-Error Note, Back

Error Note #1, Front

Error Note #2, Front

China, 1944, 1000 Yuan, P-J31
*FEN7 Punch cancelled notes with the suffix letter (N) missing from
the serial number on the right, the top note has an ink smear, and
the design element of the bottom note is shifted to the left*
Value: $150-250

Non-Error Note, Front

Error Note, Front

Error Note, Back

Bosnia and Herzegovina, 1994, 1000 Dinara, P-46
FEN7 Complete overprint inverted on face and serial number inverted on back
Value: $250-350

Non-Error Note, Back

Error Note, Front

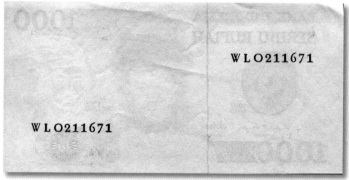

Error Note, Back

Indonesia, 1987, 1000 Rupiah, P-124a
FEN7 Design elements missing from face with the
back blank except for the serial numbers
Value: $350-500

Non-Error Note
Front and Back

MISCELLANEOUS ERRORS

Do not be fooled by this catch-all designation. Despite this innocuous description, some of the most visually impressive and significant errors illustrated in this book appear in this section. In fact, some miscellaneous errors are so unusual that they do not fall into any of the other more traditional error categories earlier described. To this end, errors of this nature are rarely seen in the paper money issued by the United States. Accordingly, some miscellaneous errors have received the highest FEN numbers.

Error Note, Front

Germany, 1921, Notgeld (Town of Lunden)
FEN8 An extremely rare double denomination bearing a 100-Mark value printed on one side and a 10-Mark value on the opposite side
Value: $1,500-2,000

Error Note, Back

Error Note, Back

Non-Error Note, Front

Cuba, 2001, 20 Pesos, P-118
*FEN8 This note has two fronts and different
serial numbers printed on opposite sides*
Value: $500-1,000

Non-Error Note, Back

Error Note #1, Back

25B 060065

Error Note #1, Front

India, No Date, 10 Rupees, P-89c
FEN7 An unusual error where a pair of sheets stuck together when printed and then separated so that the face of the first note from the top sheet only received its serial numbers and the back of the second note from the bottom sheet is blank
Value: $400-600

Error Note #2, Front

Error Note #2, Back

Error Note, Front

Non-Error Note, Front

Iraq, 1994, 50 Dinars, P-83
FEN8 Face and back designs are printed over one another
on the face with the back design normal
Value: $250-350

Error Note, Back

Error Note #1, Front

Error Note #2, Front

Paraguay, No Date, 5 Guaranies, P-195b
FEN8 Identical serial numbers printed on different notes
Value: $300-500 for the pair

Error Note, Back

Error Note #1, Front

Error Note #2, Front

Japan, No Date, 10 Yen, P-40a
FEN8 Another very uncommon pair of notes bearing identical serial numbers
Value: $200-300 for the pair

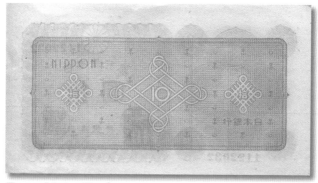

Error Note, Back

Error Notes, Fronts

Greece, 1944, 2000 Drachmai, P-133
FEN8 A small run of notes having identical serial numbers
Perhaps this is the result of a stuck final digit
Value: $300-500 for the three notes

Error Note, Back

Error Note, Front

Mexico, 1941, 20 Pesos, P-40c
FEN8 Mismatched series year (1491/1941) overprinted on face
Value: $200-300

Error Note, Back

Error Note, Front

Non-Error Note, Front

Thailand, No Date, 100 Baht, P-97
FEN5 Security strip omitted from face
Value: $150-250

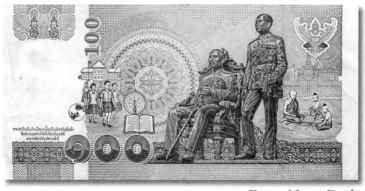

Error Note, Back

Error Note, Front

Non-Error Note, Front

Singapore, No Date, 10 Dollars, P-40
FEN5 Security foil omitted from face
Value: $150-250

Error Note, Back

 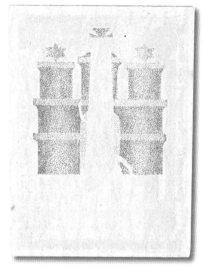

Error Note #1, Front   Error Note #2, Front

Germany, 1921, 50 Pfennig, Notgeld (Hamburg Culture and Sport)
FEN5 Error varieties showing design elements missing from the face
Value: $100-150

Non-Error Note, Front

Error Note, Front

Non-Error Note, Front

Papua New Guinea, No Date, 2 Kina, P-5c
FEN2 Large selvage retained along bottom
Value: $50-75

Error Note, Back

Error Note, Front

Non-Error Note, Front

Chile, No Date, 10 Escudos, P-139
FEN0 An error in artistic judgment, entire design hand drawn on blank face
Value: No value as an error

Error Note, Back

APPENDIX
REAL OR PSEUDO ERRORS

Iraq, No Date, 250 Dinars, P-85
Value: $400-600

On occasion, we may be fortunate to locate what appears at first blush to be a scarce and visually impressive error. But, how can one be certain that this find is truly a mistake? Even when the regular issue is available for comparison, it is sometimes difficult to determine whether we are holding a valuable error or a man made pseudo error. The ability to identify an authentic error has been complicated with the advent of high-quality color printers and software that makes it possible to capture, position, and overprint images on bank notes. In some cases, an apparent error note is neither a genuine nor a faux error. As will be illustrated in the pages to come, one or more features may have been intentionally omitted so that a partially printed note will be available for testing purposes, inspection, or to demonstrate different stages of the printing process.

Consider first the Iraqi note shown at the top of this page having what appears to be a massive cutting error (FEN 5). As described earlier in this book, a cutting error occurs when both the face and back show parts of adjacent notes. In this case, part of Saddam's head was cut off (perhaps a bad omen). While it would be easy to conclude that an unusual error is pictured above, a reliance on our visual senses alone could be misplaced.

As was also explained, most modern banknotes are printed on a sheet with the face and back of each note aligned one over the other. One example of an uncut sheet appears later in this chapter. The sheet is usually cut at the end of the production process to provide individual notes for public distribution. However, uncut sheets on which banknotes are printed are sometimes sold intact to the public. Buyers have been known to cut the sheet so that the notes, when separated, have the appearance of a cutting error. Unless we can ascertain whether uncut sheets were actually issued and the range of the serial numbers assigned to the sheet notes, it may not be possible to know if this and similar looking notes are genuine cutting errors or handmade pseudo errors.

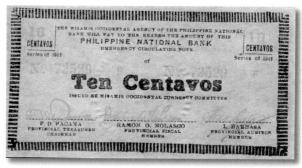

Pseudo Error Note, Front

Philippines, 1942, 10 Centavos, P-S573
Value: $100-150

Psuedo Error Note, Back

Pictured above are both sides of an Emergency Circulating Note issued in the Philippines during Japanese occupation. While this note appears bland, one cannot overlook the back which is inverted relative to the face. Few invert errors (FEN 7) have been uncovered for this book.

Once again, our senses may be fooled and our hopes of finding a truly rare error dashed. In this case, all notes from this series issued by The Misamis Occidental Currency Committee in the Philippines were printed with inverted backs (or fronts) relative to the opposite side. Despite its eye-catching appearance, the example pictured here is the normal issue, and no error is present.

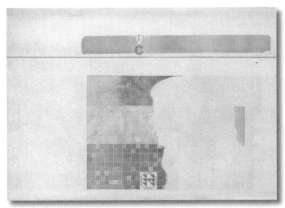

Pseudo Error Note #1, Front

Psuedo Error Note #2, Front

Croatia, 1993, 5 Kuna, P-28a
Value: $100-150

A pair of Croatian notes are shown above with the security strip and many design features missing. Do these incomplete notes reflect errors (FEN 5) as some sellers have suggested? In truth, this pair is an example of printers' waste not intended for distribution. Images like these are printed for experimental purposes and have what would be considered errors if found on the issued note shown below.

Non-Error Note, Front

Now illustrated are the face and back of a rare high denomination note issued by the National Bank of Katanga (now the Republic of Congo) which, in uncirculated condition, has been known to trade for $500 or more. Consider the value of this issue compared to the next image, where many design features, including the portrait (of Tshombe), the date and serial number, are missing from the face.

Non-Error Note, Front

Non-Error Note, Back

Katanga, 1960, 500 Francs, P-9r
Value: $500-700

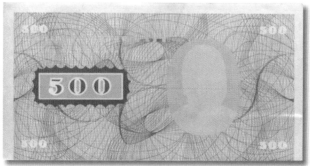

Pseudo Error Note, Front

Is this missing print (FEN 3) an error caused by the host sheet skipping a press run? Or, was the intended printing intercepted by an obstruction?

Actually, the piece demonstrated on the previous page may not be indicative of any mistake at all, but was probably an unfinished proof produced for purposes of inspection. Accordingly, the missing features are likely intentional. Such an unfinished display is often used by government printing agencies to illustrate the design features applied at different stages of the printing process.

A series of three Afghani notes also likely produced for inspection purposes is shown below. Shown first are the face and back of a normal note. The face of this regular issue was fully printed during at least three stages.

Non-Error Note, Front

Afghanistan, 1928, 10 Afghanis, P-9a
Value: $200-250 for the pair of error notes on the following page

Non-Error Note, Back

Shown now are the faces of two unfinished pieces with printings missing from each. The face of the first piece received only the first of its printings (FEN 5). The face of the second unfinished piece received its first two printings.

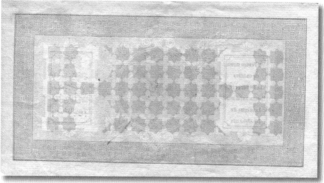

Pseudo Error Note, Front, 1st Printing

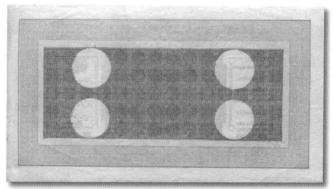

Pseudo Error Note, Front, 1st and 2nd Printings

While having the appearance of errors with missing design features similar to the Katangan example just described, the two unfinished Afghani notes are likely stage proofs or unfinished trials intentionally produced for evaluation or to demonstrate different stages of production. To this end, comparing all three faces vividly illustrates the progression of prints intended to be applied during full production. Although elegant in their appearance, the unfinished faces are devoid of errors.

Following the Afghani pieces are the faces of a pair of notes from Nepal. The first note shows the King's face looking white as a ghost. Surely, this example is illustrative of a missed printing intended to add color to the King and his wardrobe.

Pseudo-Error Note, Front #1

Non-Error Note, Front #2

Nepal, 2002, 5 Rupees, P-46
Value: $50-75

Remarkably, the face on the top note is not an error, but the actual issue designated for circulation. Because of his ghost-like image, the King objected and had the original issue recalled. The bottom note illustrates the subsequent reissue with color added to please the King and give him more life-like appearance. In a side-by-side comparison, one could reasonably conclude that the face of the first example is missing a background color or design feature (FEN 4). In reality, no error is present.

High denomination transparent polymer notes from Vietnam lie below with the first note having a blank back (FEN 4) and the second showing the regular back. The chapter in this book devoted to blank backs shows two other polymer notes with clear backs. While any error on a polymer note is rare, one should recognize that a polymer note can be altered after issue. Because of its "plastic" texture, an abrasive tool or chemical solution may be used to rub off some or all of the printing originally applied to the face or back of a polymer note to create the appearance of an error.

Psuedo Error Note, Back

Vietnam, No Date, 50,000 Dong, P-119
Value: $200-300

Non-Error Note, Back

Pseudo Error Notes, Fronts

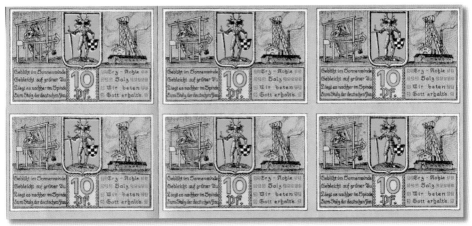

Pseudo Error Notes, Backs

Germany, 1921, 10 Pfennig, Notgeld (Town of Bleicherode)
Value: $100-150

The face and back of an uncut sheet of Notgeld are illustrated above. Amazingly, no serial number was overprinted on the face of any of the six notes on the sheet. While serial numbers missing from a single note (FEN 3) is not especially rare, the same cannot be said when an entire uncut sheet received none of its serial numbers.

Non-Error Note, Front

One example of a normal Notgeld from the same series as the uncut sheet notes is now shown with the serial number correctly applied to its face.

When considering the missing serial numbers, we must not forget the particular inflationary times during which these and other emergency issues were distributed in Germany and neighboring countries. Because of the rush to print vast numbers of Notgeld like that pictured here, the failure to apply serial numbers might be considered understandable and not completely out of the ordinary. Who can determine with certainty whether we are looking at a rare find or merely a numismatic anomaly that is of relatively little consequence?

In the portion of this book devoted to missing overprint errors, it was explained that serial numbers and signatures are examples of overprints normally applied to the face or back of a note. Sometimes a note will skip an overprint stage and not receive its serial numbers or signatures (FEN 3). Consider the faces from the pair of notes shown below issued by Martinique. The regular issue, shown second, is scarce in and of itself. The face shown first is missing its serial numbers, signatures and series designation.

Pseudo Error Note, Front

Non-Error Note, Front

Martinique, No Date, 25 Francs, P-17
Value: $300-400

In this case, care is required to distinguish a printing error from a remainder. As will be discussed in the glossary of this book, a remainder lacks certain printing features (e.g., serial numbers and signatures) that are applied to regular notes. Since it is not intended for general circulation, being able to accurately identify a remainder can be quite difficult.

An under-inked note (FEN 3) is a relatively common mistake. The normal face of a Japanese note is shown first, and the corresponding backs of two examples are presented next—the first back appearing underinked and the second being fully inked.

Non-Error Note, Front

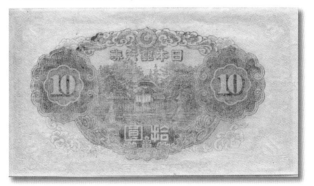

Pseudo Error Note, Back

Japan, No Date, 10 Yen, P-56b, WWII Goo Shrine note
Value: $50-75

Non-Error Note, Back

The darkness of a note varies with the ink and pressure applied to a plate. It may be that the first back is unusually underinked or simply at the low end of what would be considered normal according to contemporary standards. Whether this note is considered an error or otherwise printed within a range of acceptable darkness is a question of subjectivity.

Some or all of the notes illustrated in this section could easily become part of an advanced collection featuring world errors. Even the most studious observer cannot always distinguish real from pseudo errors. Nevertheless, because of their dramatic appearance, many pseudo errors may be worthy of our attention and understanding. In the end, no collector wishes to be fooled by paying a premium for a pseudo error purchased through inadvertence or misrepresentation.

EPILOGUE

Now that you have completed this book, I hope you will better understand my passion for collecting world paper money errors. I feel fortunate to share my enthusiasm with readers. All of the notes illustrated in this book are from my own collection or that of the Neil and Joel Shafer families. Besides the fun I had writing this book, the friendships I made while assembling my collection were an added bonus. I firmly believe that all of us, regardless of age, will benefit from a hobby. With this area of numismatics still in its infancy and waiting to expand, I encourage readers around the world to consider starting an error collection or increasing their holdings of these rare and truly fascinating notes. I look forward to personally meeting you on your numismatic journeys.

COUNTRY INDEX

GLOSSARY

To enhance your reading pleasure and understanding, provided below is a short glossary of some currency terms used in this book and not elsewhere explained.

Allied Military Currency (AMC): Notes issued by the Allied military forces (consisting of the United States, Great Britain, Russia and France) during and after World War II in Austria, France, Germany, Italy and Japan.

Double Denomination: A single note having two different numerical denominations or values printed on opposite sides.

Notgeld: Decorative emergency paper money issued primarily after World War I in large quantities usually by towns or regions in Germany and a number of other countries.

Obstruction: Typically a sheet of currency paper that is folded over itself to intercept a printing intended for the note below the fold such that the obstruction rather than the note receives the printing.

Pick Numbers: The unique catalog numbers (preceded by a "P") that are used to identify, by country, the notes illustrated in this book. The "pick" numbers have been compiled in the *Standard Catalog of World Paper Money*, a well known reference for world bank notes.

Plastic "Paper" Money: A note manufactured from a clear man-made polymer material and introduced (originally in Australia in 1988) for its superior durability and advanced security features relative to traditional paper money.

Prefix Letter(s): One or more letters appearing at the beginning of a serial number printed on a note.

Proof Note: A trial note, not typically issued for general circulation and often lacking signatures and serial numbers, produced to test the operation of a press and/or the quality and appearance of the regular printed notes.

Punch Cancelled: One or more holes punched through a note containing a production error to indicate that the note is not intended for circulation.

Remainder: A note which was partially printed but not intended to be issued into circulation. Remainders typically lack printing features such as signatures, serial numbers and dates.

Replacement Note: A note, usually designated by a special prefix letter or letters, a star or an asterisk at the beginning or end of a serial number, to replace an error that has been identified by quality control and removed prior to circulation.

Security Features: Features such as a metallic foil or strip or a special ink or water mark applied to, or incorporated in, currency paper (or plastic) to deter counterfeiting.

Selvage: Retained paper surrounding the notes printed on a currency sheet and intended to be separated and discarded after individual notes are cut from the sheet for distribution.

Solvent Smear: A note printed with "weak" or diluted ink caused by failing to completely remove a solvent applied to clean a printing plate prior to reinking.

Specimen: A sample of an original note, often having a serial number of all zeros, used to familiarize banks and government agencies with newly designed and/or issued paper money. A specimen note usually has the word SPECIMEN printed across its face.

Type II Error: A note bearing inverted serial numbers that, because of a misalignment, also shows parts of two different horizontally spaced notes. Compare this error with the more "common" Type I error having inverted serial numbers but without a misalignment showing different notes.